ICE CREAM SANDWICH COOKIE

Sensations

Easy and Fun Dessert Cookbook for Kid Chefs

Wolf Cub Chlo & Jenn Bell-Allen

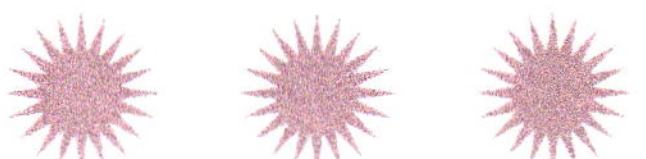

Contents

FREE Gift

Get ready for a summer full of delicious treats and unforgettable moments with our exclusive Fun Summer Activity Guide and Bonus Recipe Pack

Inside, you will discover:
- Bonus recipe pack featuring additional family-friendly, creative, and mouthwatering smoothies, popsicles, milkshakes, ice cream cookies, and more.
- Screen-Free Entertainment that encourages: Fun Outdoor Games, Entertaining crafts, Nature exploration, Social Skill Development, and much more.

If you want to create endless fun and scrumptious delights all summer long, grab your free bonuses today!

$47 Value FREE

Introducing "Sandwich Sensations"

UNLEASH YOUR INNER CHEF WITH IRRESISTIBLE SANDWICH COOKIE CREATIONS!

Are you ready to embark on a deliciously delightful adventure in the world of sandwich cookies? Look no further, because we have the ultimate treat for you and your family! Get ready to ignite your taste buds and unleash your inner chef with our exciting collection of sandwich cookie recipes.

In "Sandwich Sensations," we invite families into the whimsical world of creating mouthwatering sandwich cookies that are sure to bring joy and laughter to your kitchen. Whether you're a seasoned baking pro or just starting out, these recipes are designed with simplicity and pure enjoyment in mind, making them perfect for aspiring kid chefs and their grown-up helpers.

Our book is packed with easy-to-follow recipes that will inspire your culinary creativity. From classic combinations like chocolate chip and vanilla cream to unique flavor pairings like mint chip and double chocolate, each recipe is crafted to tickle your taste buds and leave you craving for more. But that's not all we also offer alternative in- gredient options for gluten-free, vegan, lactose-intolerant, and other dietary preferences, ensuring that everyone can indulge in these scrumptious treats.

"Sandwich Sensations" goes beyond just recipes. We've included kid-friendly measurements and vocabulary to make cooking a breeze for young chefs. Say goodbye to confusing measurements and hello to terms like handfuls, pinches, and cupcake wrappers that make it easy for kids to get involved in the kitchen. Plus, we've included a glossary of cooking terms to expand your little chef's culinary knowledge.

But the fun doesn't stop there! We've reserved some pages at the end of the book for personalization, allowing your kids to unleash their creativity. They can write down their favorite recipes, draw their own cookie illustrations, and even invent their very own sandwich cookie masterpieces. It's a book that becomes their very own culinary adventure.

So gather your aprons, assemble your ingredients, and prepare for a mouthwatering journey into the world of sandwich cookies. "Sand- wich Sensations" is the perfect companion for family baking sessions, special occasions, or simply indulging in a sweet treat together. Let's create lasting memories, one delectable cookie at a time.
Get ready to experience the wonderland of sandwich cookie sensa- tions that will bring smiles to your family's faces and fill your home with the sweet aroma of homemade delights. It's time to unleash the kid chef within and embark on a deliciously delightful journey with "Sandwich Sensations: Easy and Irresistible Fun Treats for Kid Chefs." Happy baking!

Cool regards,
Mama Wolf & Wolf Cub Chlo

Ice Cream Sandwich Cookies

Indulge in Ice Cream Cookie Heaven! Get ready for a double delight that will make your taste buds dance and your cravings scream for more. Prepare for a delicious meltdown! (Pun intended)

Choco Waffle WOW

GLUTEN-FREE OPTION

- Replace all-purpose flour with gluten-free flour blend or almond flour.

LACTOSE-INTOLERANT OPTION

- Replace butter with lactose-free butter or margarine.
- Replace milk with lactose-free milk or almond milk.

VEGAN OPTION

- Replace butter with vegan butter or coconut oil.
- Replace milk with non-dairy milk, such as almond milk or oat milk.
- Use dairy-free chocolate for melting.

MATERIALS

- Waffle iron
- Mixing bowl
- Whisk
- Wire rack
- Spoon or ice cream scoop

<table>
<tr><td>

Cooking Information

</td><td>

Prep Time: 20 Min

</td><td>

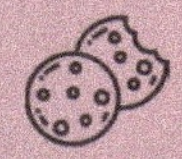

Serving: 8-10

</td></tr>
</table>

INGREDIENTS

- ½ cup of sugar (just like half a cupcake wrapper full of sugar)
- 1/4 teaspoon of salt (a tiny pinch of salt)
- ½ cup of melted butter (that's one stick of butter melted in a microwave)
- ½ cup of milk (about half a glass of milk)
- 1 teaspoon of van lla extract (a single drop of vanilla magic)
- 8 ounces of melted chocolate (about the size of a chocolate
- bar)
- Your favorite ice cream flavor (enough to fill your cookies)

DIRECTIONS

1. In a mixing bowl, whisk together the flour, sugar, and salt. Add the melted butter, milk, and vanilla extract. Stir until the batter is smooth and well combined.
2. Preheat your waffle iron according to the manufacturer's instructions.
3. Spoon about 1 tablespoon of the batter onto the center of each waffle grid. Close the lid and cook for approximately 2-3 minutes, or until the waffle cookies are golden brown and crisp.
4. Carefully remove the waffle cookies from the iron and place them on a wire rack to cool completely.
5. Once the waffle cookies have cooled, dip one side of each cookie into the melted chocolate, ensuring it is evenly coated.
6. Place the chocolate-dipped cookies back on the wire rack and allow the chocolate to set.
7. While the chocolate is setting, remove your favorite ice cream flavor from the freezer and let it soften slightly for easy scooping.
8. Take two chocolate-dipped waffle cookies and place a scoop of ice cream on the flat side of one cookie. Gently press another cookie on top to create a sandwich.
9. Repeat the process with the remaining waffle cookies and ice cream until you have the desired number of Choco-Waffle Dreamwiches.
10. For optimal texture, place the ice cream sandwiches in the freezer for at least 2 hours to firm up. Serve and enjoy these delightful Choco-Waffle Wows!

Sprinklelicious
Choco-Chipwich Delight

GLUTEN-FREE OPTION

- Replace all-purpose flour with gluten-free flour blend or almond flour.
- Use gluten-free cocoa powder.

LACTOSE-INTOLERANT OPTION

- Replace butter with lactose-free butter or margarine.
- Use lactose-free semisweet chocolate chips.

VEGAN OPTION

- Replace butter with vegan butter or coconut oil.
- Use a flaxseed or chia seed egg substitute (1 tablespoon ground flaxseed or chia seeds mixed with 3 tablespoons water) instead of the egg.
- Use dairy-free semisweet chocolate chips.

MATERIALS

- Mixing bowls
- Whisk or electric mixer
- Baking sheets
- Parchment paper
- Ice cream scoop
- Plastic wrap
- Freezer-safe container

Cooking Information

 **Prep Time:** 20 Min

 **Baking Time:** 10-12 Min

 **Chilling Time:** 1 Hour

 **Serving Size:** 6-8

INGREDIENTS

For the Double Chocolate Cookies:

- 1 cup of flour (that's about 2 handfuls of flour)
- 1/4 cup of cocoa powder (about the size of a small cupcake wrapper full of cocoa powder)
- 1/2 teaspoon of baking soda (just a little pinch of baking soda)
- 1/4 teaspoon of sa t (a tiny pinch of salt)
- 1/2 cup of softened butter (that's one stick of butter softened at room temperature)
- 1/2 cup of sugar (like filling up half of a cupcake wrapper with sugar)
- 1/2 cup of packed brown sugar (squeeze the brown sugar into a half-cup measure)
- 1 large egg (just one big egg)
- 1 teaspoon of vanilla extract (a single drop of vanilla magic)
- 1/2 cup of semisweet chocolate chips (a handful of chocolate chips)

For the Ice Cream Filling:

- 2 cups vanilla ice cream (about 2 big scoops)
- 1/4 cup sprinkles (assorted colors) (a tiny pinch)

DIRECTIONS

1. In a mixing bowl, whisk together the flour, cocoa powder, baking soda, and salt. Set aside.
2. In a separate bowl, cream together the softened butter, granulated sugar, and brown sugar until light and fluffy. Add the egg and vanilla extract, and mix until well combined.
3. Gradually add the dry ingredients to the wet ingredients, mixing until a dough forms. Stir in the chocolate chips until evenly distributed.
4. Cover the cookie dough with plastic wrap and refrigerate for at least 1 hour to firm up.
5. Preheat your oven to 350°F (175°C). Line baking sheets with parchment paper.
6. Scoop approximately 1-2 tablespoons of cookie dough and roll it into a ball. Place the cookie dough balls on the prepared baking sheets, leaving some space between each for spreading.
7. Bake the cookies for 10-12 minutes, or until the edges are set. Re-move from the oven and allow them to cool on the baking sheets for a few minutes before transferring to a wire rack to cool completely.
8. Once the cookies are completely cool, remove the vanilla ice cream from the freezer and let it soften slightly for easy spreading.
9. Take one cookie and spread a generous scoop of vanilla ice cream on the flat side. Sprinkle some colorful sprinkles over the ice cream.
10. Top with another cookie, gently pressing down to create a sandwich. Repeat the process with the remaining cookies and ice cream.
11. Place the ice cream sandwiches in a freezer-safe container, separating each layer with parchment paper. Freeze for at least 1 hour to allow the ice cream to firm up.
12. Serve and enjoy these delightful Vanilla Sprinkle Ice Cream Sandwiches with Double Chocolate Cookies!

Double Trouble

Choco Chip Ice Cream Sammies

GLUTEN-FREE OPTION

- Replace all-purpose flour with gluten-free flour blend or almond flour.
- Use gluten-free chocolate chips.

LACTOSE-INTOLERANT OPTION

- Replace butter with lactose-free butter or margarine.
- Use lactose-free chocolate chips.

VEGAN OPTION

- Replace butter with vegan butter or coconut oil.
- Use a flaxseed or chia seed egg substitute (1 tablespoon ground flaxseed or chia seeds mixed with 3 tablespoons water) instead of the eggs.
- Use dairy-free chocolate chips.

MATERIALS

- Mixing bowls
- Whisk or electric mixer
- Baking sheets
- Parchment paper
- Ice cream scoop
- Plastic wrap
- Freezer-safe container

Cooking Information

Prep Time: 20 Min	**Baking Time:** 10-12 Min	**Chilling Time:** 1 Hour	**Serving Size:** 6-8

INGREDIENTS

For the Chocolate Chip Cookies:

- 1 cup of softened butter (that's two sticks of butter softened at room temperature)
- 1 cup of granulated sugar (like filling up a whole cupcake wrapper with sugar)
- 1 cup of packed brown sugar (squeeze the brown sugar into a cup measure and press it down)
- 2 large eggs (two big eggs)
- 1 teaspoon of vanilla extract (a single drop of vanilla magic)
- 2 1/2 cups of flour (that's about 5 handfuls of flour)
- 1 teaspoon of baking soda (just a little pinch of baking soda) 1/2 teaspoon of salt (a tiny pinch of salt)
- 1 1/2 cups of chocolate chips (a handful and a half of chocolate chips)

For the Ice Cream Filling:

- 2 cups vanilla ice cream (about 2 big scoops)

DIRECTIONS

1. Preheat your oven to 350°F (175°C). Line baking sheets with parchment paper.
2. In a mixing bowl, cream together the softened butter, granulated sugar, and brown sugar until light and fluffy. Add the eggs one at a time, mixing well after each addition. Stir in the vanilla extract.
3. In a separate bowl, whisk together the flour, baking soda, and salt. Gradually add the dry ingredients to the butter mixture, mixing until just combined. Stir in the chocolate chips.
4. Scoop approximately 2 tablespoons of cookie dough and roll it into a ball. Place the cookie dough balls on the prepared baking sheets, leaving some space between each for spreading.
5. Bake the cookies for 10-12 minutes, or until golden brown around the edges. Remove from the oven and allow them to cool on the baking sheets for a few minutes before transferring to a wire rack to cool completely.
6. Once the cookies have cooled, remove the vanilla ice cream from the freezer and let it soften slightly for easy scooping.
7. Take one cookie and place a scoop of vanilla ice cream on the flat side. Top with another cookie, gently pressing down to create a sand- wich.
8. Repeat the process with the remaining cookies and ice cream to make the desired number of Double Trouble Choco Chip Ice Cream Sammies.
9. Wrap each sandwich in plastic wrap and place them in a freezer-safe container. Freeze for at least 1 hour to allow the ice cream to firm up.
10. Serve and enjoy these delectable Double Trouble Choco Chip Ice Cream Sammies!
11. Now you have a delicious recipe for Double Trouble Choco Chip Ice Cream Sammies. Indulge in the perfect combination of chewy chocolate chip cookies and creamy vanilla ice cream. They're a delight- ful treat that will satisfy your sweet tooth and bring joy to anyone who tries them!

Berry Bliss
Chocolate Chip Ice Cream Sandwiches

GLUTEN-FREE OPTION

- Replace all-purpose flour with gluten-free flour blend or almond flour.
- Use gluten-free chocolate chips.

VEGAN OPTION

- Replace butter with vegan butter or coconut oil.
- Use a flaxseed or chia seed egg substitute (1 tablespoon ground flaxseed or chia seeds mixed with 3 tablespoons water) instead of the eggs.
- Use dairy-free chocolate chips.

LACTOSE-INTOLERANT OPTION

- Replace butter with lactose-free butter or margarine.
- Use lactose-free chocolate chips.

MATERIALS

- Mixing bowls
- Whisk or electric mixer
- Baking sheets
- Parchment paper
- Ice cream scoop
- Plastic wrap
- Freezer-safe container

 **Prep Time:** 20 Min  **Baking Time:** 10-12 Min  **Chilling Time:** 1 Hour  **Serving Size:** 6-8

INGREDIENTS

For the Chocolate Chip Cookies:

- 1 cup of softened butter (that's two sticks of butter softened at room temperature)
- 1 cup of granulated sugar (like filling up a whole cupcake wrapper with sugar)
- 1 cup of packed brown sugar (squeeze the brown sugar into a cup measure and press it down)
- 2 large eggs (two big eggs)
- 1 teaspoon of vanilla extract (a single drop of vanilla magic)
- 2 1/2 cups of flour (that's about 5 handfuls of flour)
- 1 teaspoon of baking soda (just a little pinch of baking soda) 1/2 teaspoon of salt (a tiny pinch of salt)
- 1 1/2 cups of chocolate chips (a handful and a half of chocolate chips)

For the Ice Cream Filling:

- 2 cups strawberry ice cream (about 2 big scoops)

DIRECTIONS

1. Preheat your oven to 350°F (175°C). Line baking sheets with parchment paper.
2. In a mixing bowl, cream together the softened butter, granulated sugar, and brown sugar until light and fluffy. Add the eggs one at a time, mixing well after each addition. Stir in the vanilla extract.
3. In a separate bowl, whisk together the flour, baking soda, and salt. Gradually add the dry ingredients to the butter mixture, mixing until just combined. Stir in the chocolate chips.
4. Scoop approximately 2 tablespoons of cookie dough and roll it into a ball. Place the cookie dough balls on the prepared baking sheets, leaving some space between each for spreading.
5. Bake the cookies for 10-12 minutes, or until golden brown around the edges. Remove from the oven and allow them to cool on the baking sheets for a few minutes before transferring to a wire rack to cool completely.
6. Once the cookies have cooled, remove the strawberry ice cream from the freezer and let it soften slightly for easy scooping.
7. Take one cookie and place a scoop of strawberry ice cream on the flat side. Top with another cookie, gently pressing down to create a sandwich.
8. Repeat the process with the remaining cookies and ice cream to make the desired number of Berry Bliss Chocolate Chip Ice Cream Sandwiches.
9. Wrap each sandwich in plastic wrap and place them in a freezer-safe container. Freeze for at least 1 hour to allow the ice cream to firm up.
10. Serve and enjoy these delightful Berry Bliss Chocolate Chip Ice Cream Sandwiches!

Split 'n' Sandwich

Ice Cream Cookies Sandwiches

GLUTEN-FREE OPTION

- Replace all-purpose flour with a gluten-free flour blend or almond flour.
- Use gluten-free chocolate chips and vanilla chips.

VEGAN OPTION

- Replace butter with vegan butter or coconut oil.
- Use a flaxseed or chia seed egg substitute (1 tablespoon ground flaxseed or chia seeds mixed with 3 tablespoons water) instead of the eggs.
- Use dairy-free chocolate chips and vegan vanilla chips.

LACTOSE-INTOLERANT OPTION

- Replace butter with lactose-free butter or margarine.
- Use lactose-free chocolate chips and vanilla chips.
- For the ice cream filling, use lactose-free chocolate and vanilla ice cream options.

MATERIALS

- Mixing bowls
- Whisk or electric mixer
- Baking sheets
- Parchment paper
- Ice cream scoop
- Plastic wrap
- Freezer-safe container

Cooking Information

 **Prep Time:** 20 Min    **Baking Time:** 10-12 Min    **Chilling Time:** 1 Hour   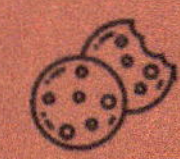 **Serving Size:** 6-8

INGREDIENTS

For the Cookies:

- 1 cup of softened butter (that's two sticks of butter softened at room temperature)
- 1 cup of granulated sugar (like filling up a whole cupcake wrapper with sugar)
- 1 cup of packed brown sugar (squeeze the brown sugar into a cup measure and press it down)
- 2 large eggs (two big eggs)
- 1 teaspoon of vanilla extract (a single drop of vanilla magic)
- 2 1/2 cups of flour (that's about 5 handfuls of flour)
- 1 teaspoon of baking soda (just a little pinch of baking soda) 1/2 teaspoon of salt (a tiny pinch of salt)
- 1 cup of chocolate chips (a handful of chocolate chips)
- 1 cup of vanilla chips (white chocolate) (a handful of white chocolate chips)

For the Ice Cream Filling:

- 2 cups chocolate ice cream (about 2 big scoops)
- 2 cups vanilla ice cream (about 2 big scoops)

DIRECTIONS

1. Preheat your oven to 350°F (175°C). Line baking sheets with parchment paper.
2. In a mixing bowl, cream together the softened butter, granulated sugar, and brown sugar until light and fluffy. Add the eggs one at a time, mixing well after each addition. Stir in the vanilla extract.
3. In a separate bowl, whisk together the flour, baking soda, and salt. Gradually add the dry ingredients to the butter mixture, mixing until just combined. Stir in the chocolate chips and vanilla chips.
4. Scoop approximately 2 tablespoons of cookie dough and roll it into a ball. Place the cookie dough balls on the prepared baking sheets, leaving some space between each for spreading.
5. Bake the cookies for 10-12 minutes, or until golden brown around the edges. Remove from the oven and allow them to cool on the baking

Confetti Funfetti
Ice Cream Cookies

GLUTEN-FREE OPTION

- Replace all-purpose flour with a gluten-free flour blend or almond flour.
- Use gluten-free baking powder.

LACTOSE-INTOLERANT OPTION

- Replace butter with lactose-free butter or margarine.
- Use lactose-free vanilla ice cream.

VEGAN OPTION

- Replace butter with vegan butter or coconut oil.
- Use a flaxseed or chia seed egg substitute (1 tablespoon ground flaxseed or chia seeds mixed with 3 tablespoons water) instead of the eggs.

MATERIALS

- Mixing bowls
- Whisk or electric mixer
- Baking sheets
- Parchment paper
- Ice cream scoop
- Plastic wrap
- Freezer-safe container

Cooking Information

 **Prep Time:** 20 Min

 **Baking Time:** 10-12 Min

 **Chilling Time:** 1 Hour

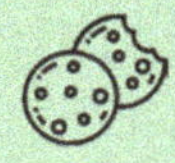 **Serving Size:** 6-8

INGREDIENTS

For the Sugar Cookies:

- 1 cup of softened butter (that's two sticks of butter softened at room temperature)
- 1 cup of granulated sugar (like filling up a whole cupcake wrapper
- with sugar)
- 2 large eggs (two big eggs)
- 1 teaspoon of vanilla extract (a single drop of vanilla magic)
- 3 cups of flour (that's about 6 handfuls of flour)
- 1 teaspoon of baking powder (just a little pinch of baking powder) 1/2 teaspoon of salt (a tiny pinch of salt)
- Colorful confetti sprinkles (as much as you like to make it colorful and fun)

For the Ice Cream Filling:

- 2 cups of vanilla ice cream (about 2 big scoops)
- Colorful confetti sprinkles (as much as you like to make it colorful and fun)

DIRECTIONS

1. Preheat your oven to 350°F (175°C). Line baking sheets with parchment paper.
2. In a mixing bowl, cream together the softened butter and granulat- ed sugar until light and fluffy. Add the eggs one at a time, mixing well after each addition. Stir in the vanilla extract.
3. In a separate bowl, whisk together the flour, baking powder, and salt. Gradually add the dry ingredients to the butter mixture, mixing until just combined.
4. Take about 1 tablespoon of dough and roll it into a ball. Flatten the ball slightly and press colorful confetti sprinkles onto the top of the cookie. Place the cookie dough on the prepared baking sheets, leaving some space between each for spreading.
5. Bake the cookies for 10-12 minutes, or until the edges are lightly golden. Remove from the oven and allow them to cool on the baking sheets for a few minutes before transferring to a wire rack to cool completely.
6. Once the cookies have cooled, remove the vanilla ice cream from the freezer and let it soften slightly for easy scooping.
7. Take one cookie and place a scoop of vanilla ice cream on the flat side. Sprinkle additional confetti sprinkles on top of the ice cream. Top with a second cookie, gently pressing down to create a sandwich.
8. Repeat the process with the remaining cookies and ice cream to make the desired number of Confetti Funfetti Ice Cream Sandwiches. Wrap each sandwich in plastic wrap and place them in a freezer-safe container. Freeze for at least 1 hour to allow the ice cream to firm up. Serve and enjoy these delightful Confetti Funfetti Ice Cream Sandwiches!

Marshmallow Nutty
Biscuit Bliss

GLUTEN-FREE OPTION

- Replace all-purpose flour with gluten-free flour blend or almond flour.

VEGAN OPTION

- Look for vegan hazelnut spread or make your own vegan chocolate hazelnut spread.
- Use vegan marshmallows made without gelatin (check for plant-based or vegan options).
- Choose vegan tea biscuit cookies or make your own vegan-friendly biscuits.

LACTOSE-INTOLERANT OPTION

- Look for lactose-free hazelnut spread or dairy-free chocolate hazel- nut spread.
- Use lactose-free or dairy-free mini marshmallows.
- Choose lactose-free tea biscuit cookies or gluten-free graham crack- ers made without lactose.

MATERIALS

- Spoon or knife for spreading
- Baking sheet (if using homemade tea biscuits)
- Parchment paper (if using homemade tea biscuits)
- Oven (if using homemade tea biscuits)
- Cooling rack (if using homemade tea biscuits)

Cooking Information

 **Prep Time:** 10 Min
(if using store-bought tea biscuits)

 **Baking Time:** 30 Min
(if making homemade tea biscuits)

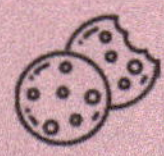 **Serving Size:** 10

INGREDIENTS

- 1 cup of hazelnut spread (like filling up a whole cupcake wrapper with hazelnut spread)
- Mini marshmallows (as many as you like, sprinkle them on top) Tea biscuit cookies (enough to make the sandwich)
- Gluten-Free Option:
- Use gluten-free hazelnut spread or chocolate hazelnut spread. Look for gluten-free mini marshmallows.
- Use gluten-free tea biscuit cookies or gluten-free graham crackers.

DIRECTIONS

If making homemade tea biscuits:

1. Preheat your oven to the temperature specified in the biscuit recipe. Prepare the tea biscuit dough according to the recipe instructions. Roll out the dough to the desired thickness and use a round cookie cutter to cut out small tea biscuits.
2. Place the tea biscuits on a baking sheet lined with parchment paper and bake according to the recipe instructions.
3. Once baked, transfer the tea biscuits to a cooling rack and allow them to cool completely.
4. Take a tea biscuit and spread a generous amount of hazelnut spread on one side using a spoon or knife.
5. Place mini marshmallows on top of the hazelnut spread, covering the entire surface.
6. Take another tea biscuit and gently press it on top of the marshmallows, creating a sandwich.
7. Repeat the process with the remaining tea biscuits, hazelnut spread, and marshmallows to create the desired number of Marshmallow Hazelnut Tea Biscuit Delights.
8. Serve and enjoy these delightful Marshmallow Hazelnut Tea Biscuit Delights!

Sprinkle Fiesta
Ice Cream Cookie

GLUTEN-FREE OPTION

- Use gluten-free all-purpose flour instead of regular all-purpose flour.
- Ensure the vanilla ice cream used for the filling is gluten-free.
- Choose gluten-free colorful sprinkles.

VEGAN OPTION

- Replace the eggs with a vegan egg substitute or use 1/4 cup unsweetened applesauce per egg.
- Use a plant-based vanilla ice cream for the filling.
- Look for vegan-friendly colorful sprinkles.

LACTOSE-INTOLERANT OPTION

- Replace the regular vanilla ice cream with lactose-free or dairy-free vanilla ice cream.
- Check the ingredients in the colorful sprinkles to ensure they are lactose-free.

MATERIALS

- Mixing bowls
- Whisk or electric mixer
- Baking sheets
- Parchment paper
- Ice cream scoop
- Plastic wrap
- Freezer-safe container

Chipper Cream Dreams

The Ultimate Vanilla Chocolate Sandwich

GLUTEN-FREE/VEGAN/LACTOSE-INTOLERANT OPTION

- 1 pint (2 cups) dairy-free vanilla ice cream
- Gluten-free chocolate chip cookies (homemade or store-bought)

MATERIALS

- Ice cream scoop
- Baking sheet
- Parchment paper or silicone mat
- Plastic wrap

<table>
<tr><td>

Cooking
Information

</td><td>

Prep Time: 10 Min

</td><td>

Serving: 4-6

</td></tr>
</table>

INGREDIENTS

- 1 p nt (2 cups) vanilla ice cream
- Chocolate chip cookies (homemade or store-bought)

DIRECTIONS

1. Allow the vanilla ice cream to soften for a few minutes to make it easier to scoop.
2. Line a baking sheet with parchment paper or a silicone mat.
3. Using an ice cream scoop, place a generous scoop of vanilla ice cream onto the flat side of one chocolate chip cookie.
4. Take another cookie and press it gently onto the ice cream, creating a sandwich.
5. Repeat the process with the remaining cookies and ice cream to make the desired number of Chipper Cream Dreams.
6. Place the sandwiches on the prepared baking sheet and cover them with plastic wrap.
7. Freeze the sandwiches for at least 2 hours, or until the ice cream is firm.
8. Serve and indulge in the ultimate vanilla-chocolate delight: Chipper Cream Dreams!

Minty Chocolate Dreamwiches

GLUTEN-FREE/VEGAN/LACTOSE-INTOLERANT OPTION

* 1 pint (2 cups) dairy-free or vegan mint chip ice cream Gluten-free or vegan soft chocolate cookies (homemade or store-bought)

MATERIALS

* Ice cream scoop
* Baking sheet
* Parchment paper or silicone mat
* Plastic wrap

Cooking Information

Prep Time: 10 Min

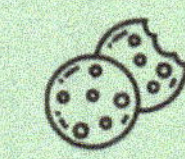

Serving: 4-6

INGREDIENTS

- 1 pint (2 cups) mint chip ice cream
- Classic soft chocolate cookies (homemade or store-bought)

DIRECTIONS

1. Take the mint chip ice cream out of the freezer and allow it to soften slightly for a few minutes to make it easier to scoop.
2. Line a baking sheet with parchment paper or a silicone mat.
3. Using an ice cream scoop, scoop a generous amount of mint chip ice cream onto the flat side of one classic soft chocolate cookie.
4. Place another cookie on top of the ice cream, flat side down, and gently press them together to create a sandwich.
5. Repeat the process with the remaining cookies and ice cream to make the desired number of Minty Chocolate Dreamwiches.
6. Place the sandwiches on the prepared baking sheet and cover them with plastic wrap.
7. Freeze the sandwiches for at least 2 hours, or until the ice cream is firm.
8. Serve and enjoy these delightful Minty Chocolate Dreamwiches!

Almond Crusted Bliss

GLUTEN-FREE/VEGAN/LACTOSE-INTOLERANT OPTION

- 1 pint (2 cups) vegan vanilla ice cream (made with almond milk or coconut milk)
- Sliced almonds
- Assorted gluten-free grains (such as crushed gluten-free cornflakes, crushed gluten-free graham crackers, or gluten-free granola)
- Vegan, gluten-free buttercream cookies (homemade or store-bought)

MATERIALS

- Ice cream scoop Baking sheet
- Parchment paper or silicone mat
- Plastic wrap

INGREDIENTS

- 1 pint (2 cups) vanilla ice cream
- Sliced almonds
- Assorted grains (such as crushed cornflakes, crushed graham crack- ers, or granola)
- Classic buttercream cookies (homemade or store-bought)

DIRECTIONS

1. Take the vanilla ice cream out of the freezer and let it soften slightly for a few minutes to make it easier to work with.
2. On a plate, spread out the sliced almonds and assorted grains. Using an ice cream scoop, scoop a generous amount of vanilla ice cream onto one side of a classic buttercream cookie.
3. Roll the ice cream side of the cookie in the sliced almonds and grains, ensuring they stick to the ice cream.
4. Take another classic buttercream cookie and press it gently onto the ice cream, creating a sandwich.
5. Repeat the process with the remaining cookies, ice cream, almonds, and grains to make the desired number of Crunchy Almond Bliss- wiches.
6. Place the sandwiches on a baking sheet lined with parchment paper or a silicone mat.
7. Cover the sheet with plastic wrap and freeze the sandwiches for at least 2 hours, or until the ice cream is firm.
8. Serve and enjoy these delightful Crunchy Almond Blisswiches!

Choco-Wafer
Swirl Delights

VEGAN/GLUTEN-FREE/LACTOSE FREE OPTION

- 1 pint (2 cups) vegan vanilla ice cream (made with almond milk or coconut milk)
- Gluten-free chocolate circular wafer cookies

MATERIALS

- Ice cream scoop or piping bag (optional)
- Baking sheet
- Plastic wrap

INGREDIENTS

- Soft serve vanilla ice cream
- Chocolate circular wafer cookies.

DIRECTIONS

1. Take the soft-serve vanilla ice cream out of the freezer and let it soften slightly for a few minutes to make it easier to work with. Line a baking sheet with plastic wrap.
2. Using an ice cream scoop or a piping bag (if available), scoop or pipe a swirl of soft-serve vanilla ice cream onto the flat side of a chocolate circular wafer cookie.
3. Place another wafer cookie on top of the ice cream, flat side down, and gently press them together to create a sandwich.
4. Repeat the process with the remaining ice cream and cookies to make the desired number of Choco-Wafer Swirl Delights.
5. Place the sandwiches on the prepared baking sheet and cover them with plastic wrap.
6. Freeze the sandwiches for at least 2 hours, or until the ice cream is firm. Whip cream is optional.
7. Serve and enjoy these delightful Choco-Wafer Swirl Delights!

GLUTEN-FREE/VEGAN/LACTOSE-INTOLERANT OPTIONS

* 1 1/2 cups gluten-free all-purpose flour or almond flour Use dairy-free or vegan butter
* Use dairy-free or vegan white chocolate chips
* For the cream filling, use vegan butter and non-dairy milk (such as almond milk or coconut milk)

MATERIALS

* Piping bag or spoon for filling
* Baking sheet
* Plastic wrap

Cooking Information

 **Prep Time:** 20 Min

 **Baking Time:** 10-12 Min

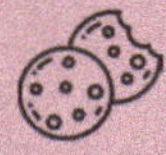 **Serving Size:** 12

INGREDIENTS

- Vanilla cream filling (homemade or store-bought) Red velvet cookies (homemade or store-bought)

Red Velvet cookies recipe:

- 1 1/2 cups all-purpose flour (fill up a cupcake wrapper flour and
- another halfway)
- 2 tablespoons unsweetened cocoa powder (2 big spoonfuls)
- 1/2 teaspoon baking soda (a pinch of baking soda)
- 1/4 teaspoon salt (a tiny pinch of salt)
- 1/2 cup unsalted butter, softened (that's one stick of soft butter)
- 3/4 cup granulated sugar (this one is a tricky one, try measuring this one)
- 1 large egg
- 1 teaspoon vanilla extract (a single drop of vanilla magic)
- 1 tablespoon red food coloring (a small spoonful of vanilla magic)
- 1/2 cup white chocolate chips (half a glass of white chocolate chips)

Ingredients for Vanilla Cream Filling:

- 1/2 cup unsalted butter, softened (that's one stick of soft butter)
- 1 1/2 cups powdered sugar (fill up a cupcake wrapper flour and another halfway)
- 1 teaspoon vanilla extract (a single drop of vanilla magic)
- 2 tablespoons milk (or non-dairy milk for vegan option)

DIRECTIONS

1. Prepare the vanilla cream filling according to the recipe or use store-bought filling for convenience.
2. Line a baking sheet with plastic wrap.
3. Preheat your oven to 350°F (175°C) and line a baking sheet with parchment paper.
4. In a medium bowl, whisk together the flour, cocoa powder, baking soda, and salt. Set aside.
5. In a large bowl, cream together the softened butter and granulated sugar until light and fluffy.
6. Add the egg, vanilla extract, and red food coloring to the butter mixture. Mix until well combined.
7. Gradually add the dry ingredients to the wet ingredients, mixing until just combined. Fold in the white chocolate chips.
8. Take small portions of dough, about the size of a ping pong ball, and roll them into balls. Place them on the prepared baking sheet, spacing them about 2 inches apart.
9. Bake the cookies for 10-12 minutes, or until the edges are set and the centers are slightly soft. Remove from the oven and let them cool on the baking sheet for a few minutes before transferring them to a wire rack to cool completely.
10. While the cookies are cooling, prepare the vanilla cream filling. In a bowl, beat the softened butter until creamy.
11. Gradually add the powdered sugar and continue beating until well combined. Add the vanilla extract and milk, and beat until light and fluffy.
12. Once the cookies are completely cooled, pair them up based on similar sizes. Take one cookie and spread a generous amount of vanilla cream filling on the flat side. Place another cookie on top, flat side down, to create a sandwich.
13. Repeat with the remaining cookies and filling.
14. Serve and enjoy these delightful Velvet Cream Swirlwiches: Red Velvet and Vanilla Delight!

S'Mores Meltdown

Marshmallow Madness

GLUTEN-FREE/VEGAN/LACTOSE-INTOLERANT OPTIONS

- Use gluten-free graham crackers or gluten-free cookies
- Use vegan marshmallows (made with plant-based ingredients)
- Use dairy-free or vegan chocolate bars or chocolate chips

MATERIALS

- Baking sheet
- Oven or microwave
- Piping bag or spoon for marshmallow and chocolate spreading

Cooking Information

 **Prep Time:** 15 Min

 **Baking Time:** 5 Min

 **Serving Size:** 12

INGREDIENTS

- 10-12 Large Marshmallows
- 4 oz Chocolate bars or chocolate chips (4 small handfuls)
- 24 Petit Beurre biscuits (or graham crackers)

DIRECTIONS

1. Preheat your oven to 350°F (175°C) or preheat a microwave-safe plate in the microwave.
2. Arrange the Petit Beurre biscuits (or graham crackers) on a baking sheet.
3. Place a marshmallow on top of each biscuit, ensuring they are evenly spaced.
4. If using an oven, carefully place the baking sheet in the preheated oven and bake for 2-3 minutes or until the marshmallows start to melt and turn golden brown. If using a microwave, heat the marshmallow-topped biscuits on the preheated plate for 10-15 seconds until the marshmallows puff up.
5. Remove the baking sheet from the oven or the plate from the microwave.
6. Immediately place a piece of chocolate on top of each melted marshmallow.
7. Take another biscuit and gently press it onto the chocolate, creating a sandwich.
8. Repeat the process with the remaining biscuits, marshmallows, and chocolate to make the desired number of S'mores Meltdowns.
9. Allow the S'mores Meltdowns to cool slightly before serving.
10. Enjoy the gooey, melty deliciousness of the S'mores Meltdowns while they're warm and enjoy the Marshmallow Madness!

Ultimate Choco-Chip
Cookie Extravaganza

GLUTEN-FREE/VEGAN/LACTOSE-INTOLERANT OPTION

- Use gluten-free chocolate chip cookies or vegan chocolate chip cookies (check for gluten-free or vegan options at your local store).
- Use dairy-free or vegan ice cream flavors (made with plant-based ingredients).
- Use dairy-free or vegan chocolate for dipping (check for dairy-free or vegan options at your local store).

MATERIALS

- Baking sheet
- Parchment paper
- Freezer-safe container or individually wrapped plastic wrap
- Piping bag or spoon for filling
- Microwave-safe bowl for melting chocolate
- Toothpicks or small forks for dipping

Cooking Information

 **Prep Time:** 30 Min

 **Freeze Time:** 2 Hours

 **Serving Size:** 12

INGREDIENTS

- Assorted ice cream flavors (such as vanilla, chocolate, strawberry,
- mint chip, etc.)
- Chocolate chip cookies (homemade or store-bought)
- Double chocolate chip cookies (homemade or store-bought)
- 8 ounces chocolate for dipping (milk, dark, or white chocolate) - (small bowful of melted chocolate)
- Colorful sprinkles

DIRECTIONS

1. Line a baking sheet with parchment paper.
2. Take a chocolate chip cookie and place a scoop of your chosen ice cream flavor on the flat side of the cookie.
3. Top the ice cream with another cookie, ensuring the flat side is facing down, to create a sandwich.
4. Repeat the process with the double chocolate chip cookies and the remaining ice cream flavors to make the desired number of ice cream sandwiches.
5. Place the ice cream sandwiches on the prepared baking sheet and transfer them to the freezer to firm up for at least 1 hour.
6. In the meantime, melt the chocolate in a microwave-safe bowl ac- cording to the package instructions, or using your preferred melting method.
7. Once the ice cream sandwiches are firm, remove them from the freezer. Dip one end of each sandwich into the melted chocolate, allowing any excess to drip off.
8. Immediately sprinkle colorful sprinkles onto the chocolate-dipped portion of the sandwiches, creating a fun and festive look.
9. Place the finished ice cream sandwiches back on the baking sheet and return them to the freezer for an additional 30 minutes to set.
10. Serve and enjoy the Choco-Chip Confetti Fiesta: Ice Cream Sand- wich Extravaganza!

Berry Brownie Bliss

GLUTEN-FREE/VEGAN/LACTOSE-INTOLERANT OPTION

- Use gluten-free brownie mix or vegan brownie mix (check for gluten-free or vegan options at your local store).
- Use dairy-free or vegan strawberry ice cream (made with plant-based ingredients).

MATERIALS

- Baking dish
- Circular cookie cutter or glass
- Parchment paper
- Freezer-safe container or individually wrapped plastic wrap

 **Prep Time:** 20 Min

 **Baking Time:** Varies

 **Chilling Time:** 2 Hours

 **Serving Size:** 12

INGREDIENTS

- Strawberry ice cream (homemade or store-bought)
- Brownie mix (homemade or store-bought)
- Fresh strawberries (optional, for garnish)

DIRECTIONS

1. Preheat your oven according to the brownie mix instructions and prepare the mix as directed.
2. Pour the brownie batter into a greased baking dish and spread it evenly.
3. Bake the brownies in the preheated oven according to the instructions.
4. Once baked, let the brownies cool completely in the baking dish. Once cooled, transfer the brownie slab onto a cutting board lined with parchment paper.
5. Using a circular cookie cutter or a glass, cut out circular shapes from the brownie slab. Aim for a size that fits well in your hand and is proportional to the ice cream.
6. Take a circular brownie and place a scoop of strawberry ice cream on top.
7. Top the ice cream with another circular brownie to create a sand- wich.
8. Repeat the process with the remaining brownie circles and straw- berry ice cream to make the desired number of ice cream sandwiches. Place the ice cream sandwiches in a freezer-safe container or indi- vidually wrap them with plastic wrap.
9. Freeze the sandwiches for at least 2 hours or until the ice cream is firm.
10. Optionally, garnish the sandwiches with fresh strawberry slices be- fore serving.
11. Serve and enjoy the Berry Brownie Bliss: Strawberry Ice Cream Sandwich Delight!

GLUTEN-FREE/VEGAN/LACTOSE-INTOLERANT OPTION

- Use gluten-free sugar wafers or gluten-free wafer-style cookies.
- Use dairy-free or vegan vanilla, strawberry, and chocolate ice cream (made with plant-based ingredients).

MATERIALS

- Baking sheet
- Parchment paper
- Freezer-safe container or individually wrapped plastic wrap

Prep Time: 10 Min

Freeze Time: 2 Hours

Serving Size: 4-6

INGREDIENTS

- Vanilla ice cream
- Strawberry ice cream
- Chocolate ice cream
- 12 Sugar wafers (store-bought or homemade)

DIRECTIONS

1. Line a baking sheet with parchment paper.
2. Place the sugar wafers on the baking sheet, evenly spaced apart. Take a scoop of vanilla ice cream and place it on one sugar wafer. Next, take a scoop of strawberry ice cream and place it on another sugar wafer.
3. Finally, take a scoop of chocolate ice cream and place it on a third sugar wafer.
4. Gently press the ice cream scoops together to create a stack, with the different flavors layered on top of one another.
5. Repeat the process with the remaining sugar wafers and ice cream flavors to make the desired number of Neapolitan Delight: Triple Ice Cream Wafer Stacks.
6. Place the stacks on the prepared baking sheet and transfer them to the freezer to firm up for at least 2 hours.
7. Once the stacks are firm, remove them from the freezer.
8. Serve the Neapolitan Delight: Triple Ice Cream Wafer Stacks as is, or for an extra touch, roll the exposed edges in colorful sprinkles, crushed nuts, or chocolate chips for added texture and fun.
9. Optionally, you can individually wrap each stack with plastic wrap for easy serving and storage.
10. Serve and enjoy the Neapolitan Delight: Triple Ice Cream Wafer Stack!

Double Chocolate

Sandwich Cookie Deluxe

GLUTEN-FREE OPTION

* Use gluten-free chocolate waffles or gluten-free chocolate cookies.

FOR VEGAN/LACTOSE-INTOLERANT OPTION

* Use dairy-free or vegan chocolate ice cream (made with plant-based ingredients).
* Use vegan chocolate waffles or cookies.

MATERIALS

* Baking sheet
* Parchment paper
* Waffle maker (if making homemade waffles)
* Knife or square cookie cutter

Cooking Information

 **Prep Time:** 15 Min

 **Baking Time:** 10 Min

 **Serving Size:** 4-6

INGREDIENTS

- Chocolate ice cream (homemade or store-bought)
- 8 Chocolate waffles (store-bought or homemade)

DIRECTIONS

1. Preheat the waffle maker according to the manufacturer's instruc- tions.
2. If using store-bought chocolate waffles, skip to step 4. If making homemade waffles, prepare the batter according to your preferred recipe or using a store-bought mix.
3. Pour the waffle batter onto the preheated waffle maker, following the recommended amount for each waffle. Close the lid and cook the waffles until they are crisp and golden brown.
4. Once the waffles are ready, let them cool completely on a wire rack.
5. Once the waffles are cooled, cut them into square shapes using a knife or a square cookie cutter. Aim for a size that is proportionate to the ice cream and fits well in your hand.
6. Take a square chocolate waffle and place a scoop of chocolate ice cream on top.
7. Top the ice cream with another square chocolate waffle to create a sandwich.
8. Repeat the process with the remaining waffle squares and chocolate ice cream to make the desired number of Choco-Waffle Delight: Dou- ble Chocolate Ice Cream Sandwiches.
9. Place the ice cream sandwiches on a baking sheet lined with parch- ment paper and transfer them to the freezer to firm up for at least 2 hours.
10. Once the sandwiches are firm, remove them from the freezer.
11. Serve the Choco-Waffle Delight: Double Chocolate Ice Cream Sandwiches as is, or for a decorative touch, dust the exposed edges with powdered sugar or drizzle melted chocolate over the top.
12. Optionally, you can individually wrap each sandwich with plastic wrap for easy serving and storage.
13. Serve and enjoy the Choco-Waffle Delight: Double Chocolate Ice Cream Sandwiches!

Berrylicious Grahamwiches

GLUTEN-FREE OPTION

- Use gluten-free chocolate graham crackers or gluten-free chocolate cookies.

VEGAN/LACTOSE-INTOLERANT OPTION

- Use dairy-free or vegan strawberry ice cream (made with plant-based ingredients).
- Use vegan chocolate graham crackers or cookies.

MATERIALS

- Baking sheet
- Parchment paper

Cooking Information

 **Prep Time:** 10 Min

 **Freeze Time:** 1 Hour

 **Serving Size:** 4-6

INGREDIENTS

- Strawberry ice cream (homemade or store-bought)
- 8 Graham crackers

DIRECTIONS

1. Take the strawberry ice cream out of the freezer and let it soften for a few minutes.
2. While the ice cream softens, line a baking sheet or tray with parch- ment paper.
3. Place 4 chocolate graham crackers on the lined baking sheet.
4. Scoop a generous amount of softened strawberry ice cream onto each graham cracker, spreading it evenly.
5. Top each ice cream-covered graham cracker with another graham cracker, creating a sandwich.
6. Gently press down to secure the sandwich together.
7. Place the baking sheet with the ice cream sandwich cookies in the freezer for at least 1 hour, or until the ice cream is firm.
8. Once the ice cream has hardened, remove the ice cream sandwich cookies from the freezer.
9. Serve the Berrylicious ice cream sandwich cookies immediately, or wrap them individually in plastic wrap and store them in the freezer for later enjoyment.
10. Serve the Berrylicious Grahamwiches: Strawberry Ice Cream Sand- wiches as is, or for an extra touch, roll the exposed edges in colorful sprinkles or crushed graham cracker crumbs for added texture and fun.
11. Optionally, you can individually wrap each sandwich with plastic wrap for easy serving and storage.
12. Serve and enjoy the Berrylicious Grahamwiches: Strawberry Ice Cream Sandwiches!

Sweet Waffle Wishes

GLUTEN-FREE OPTION

- Use gluten-free waffles or make gluten-free waffles using a gluten-free waffle mix.

FOR VEGAN/LACTOSE-INTOLERANT OPTION

- Use vegan waffles made with plant-based ingredients.
- Use dairy-free or vegan vanilla ice cream.
- Use dairy-free or vegan chocolate chips.

MATERIALS

- Baking sheet
- Parchment paper
- Microwave-safe bowl for melting chocolate
- Toothpicks or skewers
- Wax paper

Prep Time: 10 Min

Baking Time: 10 Min

Serving Size: 4

INGREDIENTS

- Vanilla ice cream (homemade or store-bought)
- 4 Plain waffles (store-bought or homemade)
- ½ cup Chocolate chips for dipping (just like half a cupcake wrapper full of sugar)
- Sprinkles

DIRECTIONS

1. Line a baking sheet with parchment paper.
2. If using homemade waffles, prepare the batter according to your using a store-bought mix. Cook the waffles in a preferred recipe waffle maker until they are golden brown and crisp. Let them cool completely.
3. Take a plain waffle and place a scoop of vanilla ice cream on one side of the waffle.
4. Place another plain waffle on top of the ice cream, creating a sandwich.
5. Repeat the process with the remaining waffles and vanilla ice cream to make the desired number of Sprinkle Fiesta Wafflewiches: Vanilla Ice Cream Delight.
6. Place the waffle sandwiches on the prepared baking sheet and trans- fer them to the freezer to firm up for at least 2 hours.
7. In the meantime, melt the chocolate in a microwave-safe bowl according to the package instructions or using your preferred method. Once the waffle sandwiches are firm, remove them from the freezer. Dip one end of each sandwich into the melted chocolate, allowing the excess to drip off. You can use a toothpick or skewer to help with the dipping process.
8. Immediately roll the dipped end in colorful sprinkles, ensuring they stick to the chocolate.
9. Place the dipped and sprinkled waffle sandwiches on wax paper or parchment paper and return them to the freezer for an additional 15 minutes to set the chocolate.
10. Once the chocolate is set, remove the Sprinkle Fiesta Wafflewiches: Vanilla Ice Cream Delight from the freezer.
11. Serve and enjoy the Sprinkle Fiesta Wafflewiches: Vanilla Ice Cream Delight!

GLUTEN-FREE OPTION

- Use gluten-free chocolate chip cookies or make gluten-free cookies using a gluten-free flour blend and gluten-free chocolate chips.

VEGAN/LACTOSE-INTOLERANT OPTION

- Use vegan chocolate chip cookies made with plant-based ingredients.
- Use dairy-free or vegan vanilla ice cream.
- Use dairy-free or vegan chocolate candies.

MATERIALS

- Baking sheets
- Parchment paper
- Ice cream scoop or spoon
- Wire rack (optional)

Cooking Information

 **Prep Time:** 15 Min

 **Baking Time:** 10-12 Min

 **Serving Size:** 6

INGREDIENTS

- Vanilla ice cream (homemade or store-bought)
- 12 Chocolate chip cookies(store-bought or homemade)
- ½ cup colored chocolate candies (like M&M's) - (just like half a cupcake wrapper full of sugar)

DIRECTIONS

1. Preheat your oven according to the chocolate chip cookie dough recipe instructions or the package instructions if using store-bought dough.
2. Line baking sheets with parchment paper.
3. Prepare the chocolate chip cookie dough according to your preferred recipe or using the store-bought dough.
4. Once the dough is ready, mix in the colored chocolate candies, such as M&M's, to add a fun and colorful twist.
5. Take a scoop of the chocolate chip cookie dough and roll it into a ball. Place it on the prepared baking sheet.
6. Repeat the process with the remaining dough, spacing the cookie dough balls a few inches apart to allow for spreading during baking.
7. Bake the cookies according to the recipe or package instructions until golden brown and slightly crisp around the edges.
8. Remove the cookies from the oven and let them cool completely on a wire rack or the baking sheet.
9. Once the cookies have cooled, remove the vanilla ice cream from the freezer to soften slightly.
10. Take one cookie and place a scoop of vanilla ice cream on the flat side of the cookie.
11. Gently press another cookie on top of the ice cream, creating a sandwich.
12. Repeat the process with the remaining cookies and vanilla ice cream to make the desired number of Colorful Chipwich Delights: Vanilla Ice Cream Sandwiches.
13. Place the ice cream sandwiches in the freezer for at least 2 hours to firm up.
14. Serve and enjoy the Colorful Chipwich Delights: Vanilla Ice Cream Sandwiches!

Macarons

Magnificient Macarons

TASTY TREATS FOR BRAVE BAKERS!

Welcome to the macaron wonderland, where sweet and colorful delights await! Macarons are special cookies that come all the way from France, where they were created many, many years ago. These little treats are known for their smooth, crunchy shells and soft, chewy centers that burst with amazing flavors.

Now, listen up, budding bakers! Making macarons can be quite a challenge, even for the bravest of kitchen adventurers. It's like a magical science experiment, where precision and patience are key. That's why I have some exciting news for you! In this book, I'll not only share some super easy recipes using pre-made macarons, but I'll also give you a chance to try your hand at a couple of advanced-level macaron recipes with the help of an adult.

You see, creating the perfect macaron requires careful measuring, gentle folding, and just the right oven temperature. It's like solving a delicious puzzle! But don't worry, I'll guide you through the process step by step, so you can unleash your baking skills and create your very own macaron masterpieces.

For those looking for a quick and delightful treat, I've got some fantastic recipes that use pre-made macarons as the star of the show. You can get creative with fillings, like fruity jams, fluffy whipped cream, or even dreamy chocolate ganache. These recipes are perfect for beginners and will satisfy your sweet tooth in no time.

But wait, there's more! If you're up for a baking challenge, I've got a couple of mind-boggling macaron recipes that will push your skills to the next level.
So get ready, my young kitchen heroes! It's time to dive into the enchanting world of macarons, where colors, flavors, and creativity collide. Prepare to embark on a delicious adventure, where even the most daring bakers can become macaron masters. Let's whip up some macaron magic and make taste buds dance with delight!

Are you excited? I know I am! Let's turn the page and uncover the secrets of these marvelous macarons together.

Macaron Pop Party

MATERIALS

- Pre-made macarons (in your favorite flavors)
- Lollipop sticks or paper straws
- Candy melts or white chocolate chips
- Food coloring (Tiffany blue)
- Sprinkles or edible decorations (optional)

Cooking Information

Prep Time: 30 Min

Creating your own macaron pops at home is a delightful way to enjoy these tasty treats with a fun twist! With pre-made macarons as your starting point, you'll be able to bring a pop of color and excitement to your macaron experience. Here's how you can recreate those stunning Tiffany blue and white macaron pops:

INGREDIENTS

- Strawberry ice cream (homemade or store-bought)
- Brownie mix (homemade or store-bought)
- Fresh strawberries (optional, for garnish)

DIRECTIONS

1. Start by gently inserting a lollipop stick or paper straw into the bottom of each macaron, taking care not to push too hard to avoid cracking the delicate shells.
2. Melt the candy melts or white chocolate chips according to the package instructions. You can use a microwave or a double boiler method to melt the chocolate.
3. Once the chocolate is melted and smooth, add a few drops of Tiffany blue food coloring and stir until you achieve the desired shade. Remember, a little goes a long way, so start with a small amount and add more if needed.
4. Holding the macaron by the stick, carefully dip the top half of the macaron into the colored chocolate, allowing any excess to drip off.
5. If desired, immediately sprinkle the wet chocolate with some col- orful sprinkles or edible decorations to add extra pizzazz.
6. Place the dipped macaron pops on a parchment-lined baking sheet or stand them upright in a block of foam to allow the chocolate to set. You can refrigerate them for about 15 minutes to speed up the process.
7. Once the chocolate is completely set and firm, your beautiful mac- aron pops are ready to be enjoyed! Serve them as a fun treat at parties, celebrations, or simply as a delightful dessert.
8. Remember, macaron pops are as much a feast for the eyes as they are for the taste buds. Get creative with different flavors, colors, and decorations to make your macaron pops truly unique and special. Whether you're enjoying them yourself or sharing them with friends and family, these delightful macaron pops are sure to bring a smile to everyone's faces!
9. Enjoy the magic of macaron pops and let your imagination soar with these whimsical treats. Bon appétit!

Flavor Fusion Macaron
Create Your Own Masterpiece

GLUTEN-FREE/VEGAN/LACTOSE-INTOLERANT OPTIONS

* Use gluten-free Macarons
* Use dairy-free or vegan ice cream.

MATERIALS

* Parchment paper
* Freezer-safe container

Prep Time: 15 Min

Creating your own macaron ice cream sandwiches at home is a delightful and delicious treat! With pre-made macarons as the base, you can easily assemble these delightful confections in no time. Here's how kids can recreate these mouthwatering macaron ice cream sandwiches:

INGREDIENTS

- Pre-made macarons (assorted flavors)
- Ice cream (your favorite flavors)
- Sprinkles or toppings (optional)

NOTE

Adult supervision may be required when handling freezing temperatures and using sharp utensils.

DIRECTIONS

1. Line a baking sheet with parchment paper for easy assembly and freezing.
2. Carefully separate the macaron shells from the pre-made macarons. Place the shells flat-side up on the prepared baking sheet.
3. Take a scoop of your desired ice cream flavor and place it onto the flat side of one macaron shell. Use the back of the spoon to spread the ice cream evenly on the surface.
4. Gently press another macaron shell on top of the ice cream, creating a sandwich. The ice cream should be sandwiched between the two macaron shells.
5. Optional: Roll the sides of the ice cream sandwich in sprinkles or other toppings of your choice to add a fun and colorful touch.
6. Repeat the process with the remaining macaron shells and ice cream until you have made as many macaron ice cream sandwiches as you desire.
7. Once all the macaron ice cream sandwiches are assembled, place the baking sheet in the freezer and let them freeze for at least 2 hours or until the ice cream is firm.
8. After the macaron ice cream sandwiches are fully frozen, transfer them to a freezer-safe container for storage if desired.
9. When you're ready to enjoy the macaron ice cream sandwiches, take them out of the freezer and let them sit for a few minutes to soften slightly before serving.
10. These macaron ice cream sandwiches are a delightful treat that combines the delicate flavors of macarons with the creamy goodness of ice cream. They make for a fantastic dessert or a special treat to enjoy with family and friends.
11. Remember to experiment with different macaron and ice cream flavors to find your favorite combinations. Get creative and have fun with your macaron ice cream sandwich creations!

Berry Sweet Adventure

ADVANCED LEVEL CHALLENGE #1

GLUTEN-FREE OPTION/VEGAN/LACTOSE INTOLERANT OPTIONS

- Use gluten-free almond flour or 1 cup finely ground gluten-free oats.
- Use vegan powdered sugar

EGG WHITES

- Substitute with 3 tablespoons aquafaba (chickpea brine) or 3 tablespoons applesauce for a vegan option.
- Substitute granulated sugar with coconut sugar or ¼ cup maple syrup

MATERIALS

- Mixing bowls
- Electric mixer or whisk
- Sifter or fine-mesh sieve
- Piping bag with a round tip
- Baking sheets
- Parchment paper
- Cooling rack

Cooking Information

Prep Time:
45 Min

Baking Time:
12-14 Min

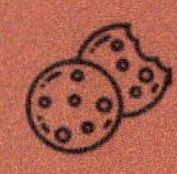

Serving Size:
24

Welcome to the advanced level of macaron mastery! Get ready to take your baking skills to the next level with this delicious Raspberry Macaron recipe. These delicate treats will impress your friends and family with their vibrant color and fruity flavor. Let's dive into the world of raspberry macarons!

INGREDIENTS

- 1 cup almond flour (enough ground almonds to fill a small cup)
- 1/4 cups powdered sugar (enough powdered sugar to fill a big cup and a little more)
- 3 large egg whites (3 big egg whites)
- 1⁄4 cup granulated sugar (a small handful of regular sugar)
- Red food coloring (optional)
- Raspberry jam or fi ling of your choice

DIRECTIONS

Preparing the Macaron Shells:

1. Line baking sheets with parchment paper and set aside. b. In a mixing bowl, sift together the almond flour and powdered sugar to remove any lumps. Set aside.
2. In a separate bowl, beat the egg whites with an electric mixer or whisk until frothy.
3. Gradually add granulated sugar to the egg whites while contin- uing to beat. Beat until stiff peaks form and the mixture is glossy.
4. If desired, add a few drops of red food co oring to achieve a vibrant pink color.
5. Gently fold the sifted almond flour and powdered sugar mixture into the beaten egg whites until well combined. The batter should be smooth and flow like lava.
6. Transfer the batter into a piping bag fitted with a round tip.

Piping and Baking the Macarons:

1. Pipe small circles onto the prepared baking sheets, spacing them about 1 inch apart. Aim for uniform sizes.
2. Once all the circles are piped, firmly tap the baking sheets on the counter to release any air bubbles.
3. Let the piped macarons sit at room temperature for about 30 minutes to develop a slight crust.

Baking and Filling the Macarons:

1. Preheat your oven to 300°F (150°C).
2. Place the baking sheets in the preheated oven and bake for 12-14 minutes until the macarons have risen and formed "feet" on the bot- tom.
3. Remove the baking sheets from the oven and let the macarons cool completely on the sheets.
4. Once cooled, carefully remove the macaron shells from the parchment paper.

Filling the Macarons:

1. Match up similar-sized macaron shells to create pairs.
2. Spoon a small dollop of raspberry jam or filling of your choice onto the flat side of one macaron shell.
3. Gently press another macaron shell on top, creating a sandwich. d. Repeat this process with the remaining macaron shells until all the macarons are filled.

Enjoying Your Raspberry Macarons:

1. Place the filled macarons in an airtight container and refrigerate for at least 24 hours to allow the flavors to meld together.
2. Take the macarons out of the refrigerator and let them come to room temperature before serving.
3. Serve your delicious raspberry macarons on a plate or platter and watch everyone's faces light up with joy!

Remember, this recipe is a challenge, and it's okay to ask an adult for help. Take your time, follow the steps, and be proud of your raspberry macarons

Choco-Mania Macarons

ADVANCED LEVEL CHALLENGE #2

GLUTEN-FREE OPTION/VEGAN/LACTOSE INTOLERANT OPTIONS

- Use gluten-free almond flour or 1 cup finely ground gluten-free oats.
- Use vegan powdered sugar

EGG WHITES

- Substitute with 3 tablespoons aquafaba (chickpea brine) or 3 tablespoons applesauce for a vegan option.
- Substitute granulated sugar with coconut sugar or 1/4 cup maple syrup

MATERIALS

- Mixing bowls
- Electric mixer or whisk
- Sifter or fine-mesh sieve
- Piping bag with a round tip
- Baking sheets
- Parchment paper Cooling rack

Cooking Information

Prep Time:
45 Min

Baking Time:
12-14 Min

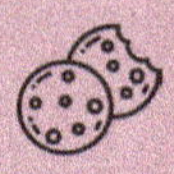

Serving Size:
24

Calling all chocolate lovers! Get ready to embark on an advanced-level baking adventure with our delightful Chocolate Macaron recipe. These decadent treats will satisfy your sweet tooth and leave you craving for more. So put on your baking hats and let's dive into the world of chocolatey goodness!

INGREDIENTS

- 1 cup almond flour
- 1/4 cups powdered sugar
- 3 large egg whites
- 1/4 cup granulated sugar
- 2 tablespoons unsweetened cocoa powder
- Chocolate ganache or filling of your choice

DIRECTIONS

Preparing the Macaron Shells:

1. Line baking sheets with parchment paper and set them aside. b. In a mixing bowl, sift together the almond flour, powdered sugar, and cocoa powder to remove any lumps. Set aside.
2. In a separate bowl, beat the egg whites with an electric mixer or whisk until frothy.
3. Gradually add granulated sugar to the egg whites while contin- uing to beat. Beat until stiff peaks form and the mixture is glossy.
4. Gently fold the sifted almond flour, powdered sugar, and cocoa powder mixture into the beaten egg whites until well combined. The batter should be smooth and flow like lava.
5. Transfer the batter into a piping bag fitted with a round tip.

Piping and Baking the Macarons:

1. Pipe small circles onto the prepared baking sheets, spacing them about 1 inch apart. Aim for uniform sizes.
2. Once all the circles are piped, firmly tap the baking sheets on the counter to release any air bubbles.
3. Let the piped macarons sit at room temperature for about 30 minutes to develop a slight crust.

Baking and Filling the Macarons:

1. Preheat your oven to 300°F (150°C).
2. Place the baking sheets in the preheated oven and bake for 12-14 minutes until the macarons have risen and formed "feet" on the bottom.
3. Remove the baking sheets from the oven and let the macarons cool completely on the sheets.
4. Once cooled, carefully remove the macaron shells from the parchment paper.

Filling the Macarons:

1. Match up similar-sized macaron shells to create pairs.
2. Spoon a small dollop of chocolate ganache or filling of your choice onto the flat side of one macaron shell.
3. Gently press another macaron shell on top, creating a sandwich. d. Repeat this process with the remaining macaron shells until all the macarons are filled.

Indulging in Chocolatey Goodness:

1. Place the filled macarons in an airtight container and refrigerate for at least 24 hours to allow the flavors to meld together.
2. Take the macarons out of the refrigerator and let them come to room temperature before serving.
3. Get ready for a chocolatey explosion of flavors as you bite into these irresistible Choco-Mania Macarons!

Remember, this recipe is an advanced challenge, and it's okay to ask an adult for assistance. Enjoy the journey of creating these delicious chocolate macarons, and dive into the chocolaty world of baking! Just remember, practice makes perfect, so don't worry if your first attempt isn't picture-perfect. Keep trying, and soon you'll become a master chocolatier! So gather your ingredients, put on your apron, and let's get started on this chocolate-filled adventure. Get ready for a taste sensation that will make your taste buds dance with joy!

Macaron Master

Design Your Own

MATERIALS

- Mixing bowls
- Spatula
- Piping bag with a round tip
- Baking sheets
- Parchment paper
- Cooling rack

Welcome to the world of Flavor Fusion Macarons, where creativity and deliciousness collide! In this recipe, we'll guide you on a journey to explore different flavors and fillings for your macarons. Whether you're a fan of zesty lime, sweet strawberry, tangy lemon, or rich chocolate, get ready to unleash your imagination and create your very own macaron masterpieces!

INGREDIENTS

- Pre-made macaron shells in assorted flavors (lime, strawberry,
- lemon, chocolate)
- Assorted fillings and toppings of your choice:
- Lemon curd
- Strawberry jam
- Chocolate ganache
- Lime zest
- Sprinkles
- Mini chocolate chips
- Optional: Food coloring (gel or powder)

DIRECTIONS

Prepare Your Fillings:

1. Gather your assorted fillings and toppings in separate bowls.
2. If desired, you can tint some of the fillings with food coloring for extra fun and creativity.

Match the Macaron Shells:
1. Sort the pre-made macaron shells into flavor pairs (lime with lime, strawberry with strawberry, etc.).
2. Lay out the matched pairs on a clean workspace.

Fill and Decorate:

1. Take one macaron shell from each flavor pair and place them side by side.
2. Choose your desired filling and spoon a small amount onto the flat side of one macaron shell.
3. Gently press the flat side of the matching macaron shell onto the filling, creating a sandwich.

4. Repeat this process with the remaining macaron shells and fill- ings, mixing and matching flavors as you go.
5. Once the macarons are filled, you can get creative with deco- rations! Sprinkle some lime zest, mini chocolate chips, or colorful sprinkles on the filling to add a pop of flavor and visual appeal.

Let Them Rest:

1. Place the filled macarons on a baking sheet lined with parchment paper.
2. Allow the macarons to rest at room temperature for about 30 minutes. This helps the flavors meld together and the shells to slightly soften.

Enjoy Your Flavor Fusion Macarons:

1. Once the resting time is complete, your Flavor Fusion Macarons are ready to be enjoyed!
2. Serve them on a platter or pack them in a cute box to share with family and friends.
3. Be sure to save some for yourself too, because these personalized macarons are truly a treat!

Now, unleash your creativity and have a blast experimenting with different flavor combinations. Remember, the sky's the limit when it comes to Flavor Fusion Macarons!

Recipe Personalization

HERE'S A FUN SECTION JUST FOR YOU!

Take a moment to personalize your cookbook and make it truly your own. Here are some fun activities you can participate in, on the following pages:

- Fun Food Facts
- Food Critic
- Ice Cream Sandwich Trivia Challenge
- My Favorite Recipes
- Draw Your Masterpieces
- Design Your Own Recipe
- Design Your Dream Ice Cream Sandwich Shop

Fun Food Facts

1. Macarons originated in France and have been enjoyed for centuries as delicate and flavorful sandwich cookies.

2. Macarons are made using almond flour, which gives them their 2 distinct chewy texture.

3. The first ice cream sandwich, as we know it today, was created in New York City in 1899 by an unknown pushcart vendor who sandwiched vanilla ice cream between two graham crackers.

4. Macaron ice cream sandwiches combine the best of both worlds, bringing together the delicate flavors of macarons and the creamy goodness of ice cream.

5. Ice cream sandwiches have different names around the world. In Australia, they are called "Monaco Bar," while in India, they are known as "Choco Bar." In Japan, they go by the name "Wafer Ice Cream," and in Mexico, they are called "Helado Sandwich."

6. Did you know that the world's largest ice cream sandwich was created in Nebraska, USA, and weighed about 3,000 pounds?

7. One of the most popular macaron flavors is pistachio.

8. Did you know that they have been enjoyed throughout history? In ancient Persia, people would sandwich ice cream between thin wafers or bread, creating a precursor to the modern-day ice cream sandwich.

9. Did you know that vanilla is the most popular ice cream flavor around the world? Right behind vanilla, chocolate ice cream takes a close second place in popularity

10. Did you know that strawberries are not only delicious but also nutritious? Strawberries are packed with vitamins and antioxidants, making them a healthy choice for your ice cream treat.

Food Critic

Ice Cream Sandwich Recipe Rating and Review

Directions:

Step 1: Choose ice cream sandwich recipes you created from the book.
Step 2: Rate the recipe based on taste, texture, appearance, and overall satisfaction using the scale provided (e.g., smiley faces or stars).
Step 3: Write a brief review sharing your thoughts and experiences with the recipe. Did you love the combination of flavors? Was the texture just right?
Get creative and decorate the page with colorful drawings or stickers to make it even more fun!
Step 4: Repeat the activity for other recipes you try and compare your ratings and reviews.

Recipe: ______________________

Taste:

- ☐ 🤢 ⭐ — Yuck!
- ☐ 🙂 ⭐⭐ — Not my favorite.
- ☐ 😛 ⭐⭐⭐ — It's okay.
- ☐ 😋 ⭐⭐⭐⭐ — Yummy!
- ☐ 😍 ⭐⭐⭐⭐⭐ — Absolutely delicious!

Texture:

- ☐ 🤢 ⭐ — Too mushy.
- ☐ 🙂 ⭐⭐ — A bit weird.
- ☐ 😛 ⭐⭐⭐ — Just right.
- ☐ 😋 ⭐⭐⭐⭐ — Nice and smooth.
- ☐ 😍 ⭐⭐⭐⭐⭐ — Perfectly creamy!

Appearance:

- ☐ 🤢 ⭐ — Not appetizing.
- ☐ 🙂 ⭐⭐ — It looks okay.
- ☐ 😛 ⭐⭐⭐ — Pretty good.
- ☐ 😋 ⭐⭐⭐⭐ — Looks scrumptious!
- ☐ 😍 ⭐⭐⭐⭐⭐ — Absolutely beautiful!

Overall Satisfaction:

- ☐ 🤢 ⭐ — Disappointed.
- ☐ 🙂 ⭐⭐ — Just okay.
- ☐ 😛 ⭐⭐⭐ — Satisfactory.
- ☐ 😋 ⭐⭐⭐⭐ — Very happy!
- ☐ 😍 ⭐⭐⭐⭐⭐ — Absolutely loved it!

Review:

* Remember to have fun, be honest, and share your opinions as you become a food critic for these delightful ice cream sandwich recipes!

Recipe: ___________________

Taste:

- ☐ 🤢 ⭐ Yuck!
- ☐ 🙂 ⭐⭐ Not my favorite.
- ☐ 😛 ⭐⭐⭐ It's okay.
- ☐ 😋 ⭐⭐⭐⭐ Yummy!
- ☐ 😍 ⭐⭐⭐⭐⭐ Absolutely delicious!

Texture:

- ☐ 🤢 ⭐ Too mushy.
- ☐ 🙂 ⭐⭐ A bit weird.
- ☐ 😛 ⭐⭐⭐ Just right.
- ☐ 😋 ⭐⭐⭐⭐ Nice and smooth.
- ☐ 😍 ⭐⭐⭐⭐⭐ Perfectly creamy!

Appearance:

- ☐ 🤢 ⭐ Not appetizing.
- ☐ 🙂 ⭐⭐ It looks okay.
- ☐ 😛 ⭐⭐⭐ Pretty good.
- ☐ 😋 ⭐⭐⭐⭐ Looks scrumptious!
- ☐ 😍 ⭐⭐⭐⭐⭐ Absolutely beautiful!

Overall Satisfaction:

- ☐ 🤢 ⭐ Disappointed.
- ☐ 🙂 ⭐⭐ Just okay.
- ☐ 😛 ⭐⭐⭐ Satisfactory.
- ☐ 😋 ⭐⭐⭐⭐ Very happy!
- ☐ 😍 ⭐⭐⭐⭐⭐ Absolutely loved it!

Review:

* Remember to have fun, be honest, and share your opinions as you become a food critic for these delightful ice cream sandwich recipes!

Recipe: ________________________

Taste:

☐ 🤮 ⭐		Yuck!
☐ 🙂 ⭐⭐		Not my favorite.
☐ 😋 ⭐⭐⭐		It's okay.
☐ 😊 ⭐⭐⭐⭐		Yummy!
☐ 😍 ⭐⭐⭐⭐⭐		Absolutely delicious!

Texture:

☐ 🤮 ⭐		Too mushy.
☐ 🙂 ⭐⭐		A bit weird.
☐ 😋 ⭐⭐⭐		Just right.
☐ 😊 ⭐⭐⭐⭐		Nice and smooth.
☐ 😍 ⭐⭐⭐⭐⭐		Perfectly creamy!

Appearance:

☐ 🤮 ⭐		Not appetizing.
☐ 🙂 ⭐⭐		It looks okay.
☐ 😋 ⭐⭐⭐		Pretty good.
☐ 😊 ⭐⭐⭐⭐		Looks scrumptious!
☐ 😍 ⭐⭐⭐⭐⭐		Absolutely beautiful!

Overall Satisfaction:

☐ 🤮 ⭐		Disappointed.
☐ 🙂 ⭐⭐		Just okay.
☐ 😋 ⭐⭐⭐		Satisfactory.
☐ 😊 ⭐⭐⭐⭐		Very happy!
☐ 😍 ⭐⭐⭐⭐⭐		Absolutely loved it!

Review:

* Remember to have fun, be honest, and share your opinions as you become a food critic for these delightful ice cream sandwich recipes!

Recipe: _______________________

Taste:

☐ 😖 ⭐ Yuck!
☐ 🙂 ⭐⭐ Not my favorite.
☐ 😛 ⭐⭐⭐ It's okay.
☐ 😋 ⭐⭐⭐⭐ Yummy!
☐ 😍 ⭐⭐⭐⭐⭐ Absolutely delicious!

Texture:

☐ 😖 ⭐ Too mushy.
☐ 🙂 ⭐⭐ A bit weird.
☐ 😛 ⭐⭐⭐ Just right.
☐ 😋 ⭐⭐⭐⭐ Nice and smooth.
☐ 😍 ⭐⭐⭐⭐⭐ Perfectly creamy!

Appearance:

☐ 😖 ⭐ Not appetizing.
☐ 🙂 ⭐⭐ It looks okay.
☐ 😛 ⭐⭐⭐ Pretty good.
☐ 😋 ⭐⭐⭐⭐ Looks scrumptious!
☐ 😍 ⭐⭐⭐⭐⭐ Absolutely beautiful!

Overall Satisfaction:

☐ 😖 ⭐ Disappointed.
☐ 🙂 ⭐⭐ Just okay.
☐ 😛 ⭐⭐⭐ Satisfactory.
☐ 😋 ⭐⭐⭐⭐ Very happy!
☐ 😍 ⭐⭐⭐⭐⭐ Absolutely loved it!

Review:

* Remember to have fun, be honest, and share your opinions as you become a food critic for these delightful ice cream sandwich recipes!

Recipe: ___________________

Taste:

☐	🤢 ⭐		Yuck!
☐	🙂 ⭐⭐		Not my favorite.
☐	😋 ⭐⭐⭐		It's okay.
☐	😋 ⭐⭐⭐⭐		Yummy!
☐	😍 ⭐⭐⭐⭐⭐		Absolutely delicious!

Texture:

☐	🤢 ⭐		Too mushy.
☐	🙂 ⭐⭐		A bit weird.
☐	😋 ⭐⭐⭐		Just right.
☐	😋 ⭐⭐⭐⭐		Nice and smooth.
☐	😍 ⭐⭐⭐⭐⭐		Perfectly creamy!

Appearance:

☐	🤢 ⭐		Not appetizing.
☐	🙂 ⭐⭐		It looks okay.
☐	😋 ⭐⭐⭐		Pretty good.
☐	😋 ⭐⭐⭐⭐		Looks scrumptious!
☐	😍 ⭐⭐⭐⭐⭐		Absolutely beautiful!

Overall Satisfaction:

☐	🤢 ⭐		Disappointed.
☐	🙂 ⭐⭐		Just okay.
☐	😋 ⭐⭐⭐		Satisfactory.
☐	😋 ⭐⭐⭐⭐		Very happy!
☐	😍 ⭐⭐⭐⭐⭐		Absolutely loved it!

Review:

* Remember to have fun, be honest, and share your opinions as you become a food critic for these delightful ice cream sandwich recipes!

Recipe: ________________________

Taste:

- ☐ Yuck!
- ☐ Not my favorite.
- ☐ It's okay.
- ☐ Yummy!
- ☐ Absolutely delicious!

Texture:

- ☐ Too mushy.
- ☐ A bit weird.
- ☐ Just right.
- ☐ Nice and smooth.
- ☐ Perfectly creamy!

Appearance:

- ☐ Not appetizing.
- ☐ It looks okay.
- ☐ Pretty good.
- ☐ Looks scrumptious!
- ☐ Absolutely beautiful!

Overall Satisfaction:

- ☐ Disappointed.
- ☐ Just okay.
- ☐ Satisfactory.
- ☐ Very happy!
- ☐ Absolutely loved it!

Review:

* Remember to have fun, be honest, and share your opinions as you become a food critic for these delightful ice cream sandwich recipes!

Recipe: ______________________

Taste:

- ☐ Yuck!
- ☐ Not my favorite.
- ☐ It's okay.
- ☐ Yummy!
- ☐ Absolutely delicious!

Texture:

- ☐ Too mushy.
- ☐ A bit weird.
- ☐ Just right.
- ☐ Nice and smooth.
- ☐ Perfectly creamy!

Appearance:

- ☐ Not appetizing.
- ☐ It looks okay.
- ☐ Pretty good.
- ☐ Looks scrumptious!
- ☐ Absolutely beautiful!

Overall Satisfaction:

- ☐ Disappointed.
- ☐ Just okay.
- ☐ Satisfactory.
- ☐ Very happy!
- ☐ Absolutely loved it!

Review:

* Remember to have fun, be honest, and share your opinions as you become a food critic for these delightful ice cream sandwich recipes!

Ice Cream Sandwich Trivia Challenge

1. What year is credited with the invention of the modern ice cream sandwich?

a) 1855
b) 1899
c) 1928
d) 1963

2. What U.S. city popularized the ice cream sandwich in the 1970s?

a) Los Angeles
b) Boston
c) Philadelphia
d) New York City

3. Which two cookies are traditionally used to make an ice cream sandwich?

a) Chocolate chip cookies
b) Oatmeal cookies
c) Sugar cookies
d) Gingerbread cookies

4. In the United Kingdom, what term is often used to refer to an ice cream sandwich?

a) Frozen feast
b) Ice cream wafer
c) Frozen treat
d) Ice cream sammie

5. Which flavor of ice cream is commonly found in classic ice cream sandwiches?

a) Vanilla
b) Chocolate
c) Strawberry
d) Mint chocolate chip

6. What is the most popular ice cream sandwich shape?

a) Rectangle
b) Circle
c) Triangle
d) Square

7. What famous ice cream brand introduced the first mass-produced ice cream sandwich?

a) Ben & Jerry's
b) Häagen-Dazs
c) Baskin-Robbins
d) Good Humor

8. What country claims to have invented the "brutti e buoni" cookie sandwich, a precursor to the ice cream sandwich?

a) Italy
b) France
c) Spain
d) Greece

9. Which U.S. state is known for its ice cream sandwich festival?

a) California
b) New York
c) Wisconsin
d) Texas

10. What is the record for the world's largest ice cream sandwich, according to Guinness World Records?

a) 5 feet long (1.5m)
b) 10 feet long (3m)
c) 20 feet long (6m)
d) 34 feet long (10m)

* Remember to keep track of your answers and check them at the end to see how well you know your ice cream sandwich trivia!

Answers: 1) b., 2) d, 3)a, 4)b, 5)a, 6)a, 7)d, 8)a, 9)c, 10)d

My Favorite Recipes

Write down your favorite sandwich cookie recipes from the book or create your own unique recipes. Don't forget to add your special twists and creative ideas!

My Favorite Recipes

Write down your favorite sandwich cookie recipes from the book or create your own unique recipes. Don't forget to add your special twists and creative ideas!

My Favorite Recipes

Write down your favorite sandwich cookie recipes from the book or create your own unique recipes. Don't forget to add your special twists and creative ideas!

Draw Your Masterpieces

Use these blank pages to draw colorful illustrations of your favorite sandwich cookies. Let your imagination run wild and bring your cookie creations to life!

Draw Your Masterpieces

Use these blank pages to draw colorful illustrations of your favorite sandwich cookies. Let your imagination run wild and bring your cookie creations to life!

Design Your Own Recipe

Get creative and design your very own sandwich cookie recipe. Draw the ingredients, write the steps, and imagine the delicious flavors you want to combine. Who knows, your recipe might become a new family favorite!

Design Your Own Recipe

Get creative and design your very own sandwich cookie recipe. Draw the ingredients, write the steps, and imagine the delicious flavors you want to combine. Who knows, your recipe might become a new family favorite!

Design Your Own Recipe

Get creative and design your very own sandwich cookie recipe. Draw the ingredients, write the steps, and imagine the delicious flavors you want to combine. Who knows, your recipe might become a new family favorite!

Design Your Dream Ice Cream Sandwich Shop

Directions: Draw your Dream Ice Cream shop. Be sure to include as many details as possible like an eye-catching sign, an inviting storefront, and display cases filled with delectable ice cream sandwiches. Oh, and don't forget cozy outdoor seating, colorful decorations, or even a catchy shop name. The sky is the limit!

Kid Chef Cooking Glossary

Baking Soda: A tiny bit of a special powder that helps the cookies get bigger and fluffier when they bake.

Chocolate Chips: Little pieces of chocolate that melt and become gooey when the cookies bake. They add bursts of chocolatey goodness!

Cocoa Powder: It's a fine, brown powder that tastes like rich choco- late. It gives the cookies a yummy chocolate flavor.

Egg: A small oval-shaped ingredient that helps hold the cookies together. When we crack it open, we use the slimy inside part.

Flour: It's a soft and powdery ingredient that helps make the cookies stick together. It's like the glue that holds them in shape.

Granulated Sugar: It's a sweet ingredient that makes the cookies taste sugary. It looks like tiny crystals and adds sweetness.

Hazelnut Spread: It's a yummy and smooth chocolate spread made with nuts called hazelnuts. It tastes like a nutty chocolate dream!

Melted Butter: When we heat butter until it turns into a liquid, it becomes melted butter. It's easy to mix and adds a rich flavor to the cookies.

Melted Chocolate: When we heat chocolate until it becomes smooth and runny, it's melted chocolate. It makes the cookies extra chocolaty and gooey.

Mini Marshmallows: These are tiny, fluffy candies that are soft and squishy. They melt a little when baked and add a sweet and fluffy texture.

Packed Brown Sugar: Brown sugar that's pressed tightly into a mea- suring cup. It's sweet and has a slight caramel flavor.

Salt: A tiny amount of a special ingredient that adds a little bit of flavor to the cookies. It makes them taste even better!

Semisweet Chocolate Chips: Just like chocolate chips, but they are a little less sweet. They give the cookies a rich and deep chocolate taste.

Softened Butter: When butter is left at room temperature until it becomes soft and easy to mix, it's called softened butter. It blends well with other ingredients.

Sugar: It's a sweet ingredient that makes the cookies taste sugary. It comes in different forms, like granulated sugar and brown sugar.

Tea Biscuit Cookies: These are round cookies that are similar to graham crackers. They have a crispy texture and are great for making cookie sandwiches.

Vanilla Extract: It's a special liquid that adds a sweet and yummy flavor called vanilla. Just a few drops make the cookies taste even better.

Wafers: These are thin and crispy cookies that come in different flavors. They are perfect for making cookie sandwiches, like the ones you find in ice cream shops.

Final Note

We hope you have enjoyed a ton of frozen treats to keep you cool during those blistering hot days. If you enjoyed this book and can spare a moment of your time we would greatly appreciate your review of the book on Amazon or the site you made the purchase. It would mean the world to us and would help others find the book as well.